In the Ring

with heels on

Domestic and other Violence

Timothy White Sr.

In the Ring with Heels On © 2016 by Timothy White, Sr.

For information contact:
info@uptownmediaventures.com

Book and Cover design by Tim White Publishing

ISBN: 978-1-68121-105-3

10 9 8 7 6 5 4 3 2 1

Table of Contents

In the Ring with Heels On

Pre-fight Analysis

Before every main event fight there is what is called the Pre-fight analysis. This is done to help give insight into the fighter's history, their wins, losses, and even some personal background information that might be of interest to those who want to see the fight.

People are interested in knowing as much as possible about the fighters entering the ring, to see if they are backing, and supporting the right fighter. This is valuable information to have.

Everyone has a history, a past that speaks loudly to others and information that is public record and can be found with little help if desired to know.

This book is about domestic, and other violence, a subject that has a horrid history, and is on the increase.

The information contained in this book can do nothing to prevent this violence, if all we do is see words that we can agree on. But follow up with zero action.

There are numerous institutes that can help, but many are flawed because of bureaucracy, and a "let's wait and see what happens" mentality, or simply lack of funding. There are some matters more important than money and notoriety.

To analyze, see or be made aware of a problem such as domestic violence does not solve it. There has been more money put into analyzing problems and situations than preventing them in the first place.

As quiet as it's kept, there are fights that can be prevented long before they escalate into violence, but there must be a willingness to be proactive, rather than reactive.

To analyze is to study a matter carefully, or simply put, to give a breakdown of events before they take place. Who would not be willing to know the outcome before it takes place? Sadly, many individuals believe they are always the exception to the rule, and what happened to someone else will not happen to them.

What leads someone to believe it's necessary to prove a point by a show of violence, even putting themselves in harm's way to do so?

Getting into a ring and fighting, requires self-examination, and this book can be helpful with this process. The question of why this fight is thought to be the best or needed solution to end conflict is open to discussion.

If you are going to fight or insist that you climb

into the ring, it's important that you learn as much about your opponent as possible for your own safety.

Introduction

One of the greatest problems facing the United States, and the world is that of domestic violence. A time when there are thousands of women who have suffered violence at the hands of individuals who make the boast of loving the very people they hurt.

What is it that makes a boyfriend, or husband consider violence as the best way to communicate to one they claim to love?

Love, the word that is often thrown around as the reason for rage filled attacks, that is at times followed by regret.

What's love got to do with it? A question that many are beginning to ask, as it is the reason numerous individual's claim to be at the heart of what they do. It's either love or lack thereof.

This book will take a close look at some of the issues that take place in the homes and hearts of those who have suffered from domestic violence. I am not a doctor, nor am I suggesting I have all of the answers, but this much is certain, we cannot continue to sit idly by, and continue to ignore what is so clearly set before us.

What will it take before we take action that is not

fear or financially motivated?

True love takes action, and as we have always heard and learned, "action speaks louder than words."

Domestic violence is not going away, and it continues to build steam as long as we take the "see nothing, say nothing" approach.

In this book you will find statistics, and firsthand accounts from individuals who have been abused, or know someone who has been abused, and was willing to share their story of strength, survival, and sadly even death.

Domestic violence is not a disease, it's a deliberate act of aggression that can be stopped, but only if acted on immediately.

What good is information without application? Information alone does not solve problems. But it does highlight the need for immediate change.

Round 1
The Hype

We've all heard things that were not necessarily true, but due to the person sharing the conversation with us, and their passion for what they were saying, we often tend to believe them, and even accept what they say as being fact.

What do we base the acceptance of their words on, it's often previous examples they have given?

An example of this can be seen in one of the greatest fighters of all time, whose name was Cassius Marcellus Clay Jr. Who would later change his name to Muhammad Ali.

Muhammad Ali would go on to become one of the most well-known boxers in the world.

What you might be wondering is what does he have to do with this book and this writing? Muhammad Ali was also one of the best hype men for himself. What is hype? Hype is said to be

1. Excessive publicity.
2. Exaggerated or extravagant claims made.
3. An advertising or promotional ploy. And
4. Something deliberately misleading; a

deception.

For fighters number 4 is the one the greatest amount of focus is given.

But first, as we mentioned Muhammad Ali who was his own hype man, his hype was based on his boxing experience and his ability to deliver on his promised word of regularly predicting when he would defeat an opponent.

Hype is about deception and deliberately steering people away from what is actually taking place, something often not there, and when it comes to domestic violence it's the ability to tell and convince others by lies, and controlling the path of conversation and thought that what you believed to be there, it is also not there or true.

As we are talking about domestic violence let's not lose sight of what it's all about and that is control, from beginning to end.

Before the fighters entered into the square circle, they would go before the press and begin to trash talk one another, and exchange verbal put downs.

For some fighters, it's all about hyping themselves, and getting more people to tune in and attend, to add more money to what is called "THE PURSE".

For some individuals hype is just harmless bantering, but for others it's serious and intentionally hurtful.

Muhammad Ali would taunt his opponents with talk that would often get under their skin, and make them respond emotionally to his words, becoming upset and a few of them would react aggressively or violently.

Part of the hype is to get into the head of the other person and to see where they are weak and exploit the weakness.

There are some fighters who have promoters for the purpose of creating a buzz for their fighter. The promoter is someone who knows their fighter, they have spent time with them, and around them, and are familiar with their personality as well as their attitude.

The job of the promoter is to also hype their boxer, to make them appear larger than life, and encouraging people to come out and see their fighter destroy the opponent in the ring.

Art often imitates life, and not always in a positive way. In the times that we live it's clear that culturally, violence has increased in our nation. A great deal of which comes by way of promoting it through various means such as, movies, TV, music and social media.

Of course, some will differ on some points, but you can decide for yourself as you continue to read, and see the statistics you will find herein, and decide what you believe is true.

Hype is building up for what is to come, what that build up might be we are not sure it depends on what's in the fighter or in this case the abusers mind. But from all we know and understand, violence is on the increase on the streets, and on the road, through things such as road rage, and in the home with domestic violence and abuse.

Hype is built around what could possibly take place based on what has happened in the past.

To exploit an opponent a good fighter is required to get to know about their strengths if there are any to be found, but certainly the weaknesses of an opponent, if they are to win their fight.

In the ring with heels on is a study of possible things that lead up to fights, or what might cause them (the abused), to learn from the results of entering the ring.

The hype is a fundamental part of the fight. It sets the stage and tells us what we might expect from the fighters in the upcoming rounds.

Certainly, hyping a fight does not say who will be

the winner, but it calls attention to the fight, as well as the fighters, and what to look forward to once the fight has begun.

Hype is an act of bragging and boasting of one's ability to defeat an opponent who gets in the ring.

The Deception

What is it that makes someone believe they can overcome years, or a lifetime of negative and bad habits? When it comes to relationships, somehow this becomes the thinking of those entering into them, that somehow, they can change a bad habit or another individual.

Life is about change, constantly changing, and making mental modifications in one's personal life.

There's a thinking that women and men have that somehow, they have the ability to magically corral, harness, and tame what's inside another individual.

More to the point there is a willful blindness and sometimes ignorance that is associated with people who believe they have the right to force change on others in a relationship, this is a mindset developed by personal perception and accompanied by self-deception.

Over the years as a speaker, counselor, and minister I have found that those who sat across from me have a distorted view of what a relationship is, and what it takes to be in one.

Many of us have received our training by way of

movies, TV, and hopes and dreams. Reality is not so easy.

It's difficult to get individuals to seek therapy or counseling when they don't believe there is anything wrong, or even worse, to hide what they are going through because of the embarrassment they feel might be associated with knowing they were not as aware of situations or circumstances that confronted them, and were not as strong as they thought they were.

So, let's take a look at some of the thought process that often accompanies this type of deception.

Yes, **deception is a process**, it doesn't just happen, there are things that lead up to it and why it becomes successful. You notice that this book is describing things in boxing terms and it will become clearer as we go along why this is so.

When it comes to deception, there are two views we must examine, one**, her deception**, and two, **his deception**, and then how each have a role in the direction the relationship will go because of it.

Deception is defined in a number of ways, it's deceit, a falsehood, and misrepresentation. But the bottom line, it's a willful lie.

Why would anyone entering into a new

relationship want to lie to themselves, or to their partner, unless they intend to do them harm emotionally or physically?

People lie in order to hide the truth, and in this case the truth about themselves or their past.

Deception has become an acceptable aspect of our lives as many of us use it to get what we want from life.

Deception is presenting something, someone, or ourselves not in an altogether truthful light.

Deception is hiding the truth from those who have a right to know it. In a blossoming relationship, we tend to think there's no harm in keeping things to ourselves, or releasing information purely on a need to know basis, after all, what harm could there be? Surprisingly, there are some women who in spite of prior information gathered, and should be heeded, will do the opposite, and allow themselves through self-deception, to do what in good conscious should be avoided.

It's in the outset of moving from single to couple that extreme caution should be used but is most often ignored.

There was a time that past experiences or deeds of the past would be concealed and said to be none of your business, but if it's something that will affect a relationship it should be talked about.

Most relationships are based on either looks (for men) or loneliness (for women) or a combination of the two.

Women will see, and have what I call **RED FLAG MOMENTS**, and for the sake of desiring companionship, will in their own minds devise ways to justify making a red flag, stop moment, into a go sign.

The deception has now successfully begun. At this point, it has nothing to do with what the man wants, but what the woman is seeking.

Some of what I am saying might come across as harsh but it's true, nonetheless.

Consider this as well. Women are taught to think they should get married and have children, be a good wife, stay at home and raise the children, while the man goes out and brings home the bacon.

I know this might seem laughable in light of the way things are done today, but there are women seeking this lifestyle, so, have they been deceived? Not necessarily, this thinking is where they believe they will find security, joy, and comfort, but this is not always a realistic expectation.

Security and comfort. This is what women want

in a relationship, and they seek this more than love, and in fact they believe love is when they are secure and comfortable and have need of nothing and feel safe. This also is deceptive.

The truth hurts, but it's also very liberating if it can be accepted. Here's the thing about deception, it's often self-imposed, and we will speak more to this in upcoming chapters.

Another deception is that of not seeing the person in the relationship as an individual, but property.

The perceived thinking is that once in a relationship you stop being an individual.

A relationship does not mean you lose self-identity, relationships becomes one of inclusion, not exclusion.

Relationships are about setting up individual and personal boundaries for one's self, not limits that are forced on another individual.

Some of the confused thinking in some relationships comes from what they think the bible tells them when it says, that "the two shall become one flesh". Does this mean the two parties are no longer individuals? Certainly not.

The bible is often cited as the reason that one or the other no longer has personal or individual rights, and that marriage somehow dissolves all past ties.

As a minister on more than one occasion I've had to address this misinformation and misrepresentation of what is said and meant.

You don't and shouldn't lose your own identity, but you have a new focus, but make no mistake about it, it should not be your only focus.

Deceptions path is paved with the objectionable thinking "it's all about me".

Entering the ring of life, it's important to know what might be ahead and learn to prepare as best you can for what could possibly take place.

Bear in mind also, there are things that come in our lives that we should with swiftness of mind, and actions discard.

Self-deception is to knowingly ignore what is clearly set before you and refuse to investigate those red flag moments. What do I mean, it's those conversations with others and self that says, "I know what I'm doing."

Words that have come to be proven untrue on a daily basis. Deception is a con game, a battle of wits, a challenge to see how good the person is at concealment.

Lying is a practiced skill, the more one does it the better they presume they are at doing it. Deception is also built around hope, it's hoping the lie can be delivered and accepted without opposition.

Some men use deception, to hopefully snag the woman they want, even if it's just for the benefit of a sexual encounter, and control over them physically or emotionally.

One of the greatest tools of deception is **verbal manipulation through communicative misdirection,** or saying what people want to hear, during times of stress, confusion or uncertainty.

Deception can come from what we believe to be true, hope to be true, and not what is actually true.

The house of deception is built around hype and hope. A fighter knows what must be done from the beginning to end, if they are to be given the title winner.

They have an agenda and an endgame from the onset.

If they say the right thing, in the right way, at the right time, what they seek to achieve is almost certain, but if not, there are other options they can, and will turn to.

Round 3
The Denial

One would imagine that deception or being deceived would be difficult, and many of us would like to believe we can't be fooled, but it's this very thinking that opens us up to deception, but the accompanying danger is that of not accepting the facts as presented, and choose denial, rather than acknowledgment. Denial is not about others fooling us, but our fooling ourselves.

There have been many boxers who have entered into the ring ill prepared, individuals who did not train for the fight, or simply believed they could handle their opponent without much difficulty.

Any and everything in life requires preparation and practice even something seemingly as simple as a relationship. Be mindful, the heart and soul of this book is relationships and what should be done entering into one.

In this round 3 we find denial, a mental defensive mechanism used to reject any other possibility as fact other than the one the individual chooses to believe or accept.

How does denial differ from deception, very simply, deception comes before the act, and denial comes after the action has taken place, requiring a decision to be made before moving further, in a word, it's UNBELIEF, or REJECTION.

Denial is knowingly rejecting facts as lies, it's seeking to make what is admittedly a known wrong acceptable by way of emotional desire.

It's that "I DON'T BELIEVE YOU" attitude. Domestic violence is built on, and around denial as we will reveal in the course of this book.

A woman in denial is emotionally challenged and driven by her feelings, and not facts. She sees according to her heart, that is, her emotional mindset, and once her emotions are released, she sees just, and only what she wants to see, and believes accordingly.

We are told to never judge a book by its cover, but we're not talking about the cover but its content.

Some women tend to ignore the content (the man's mentality) because the cover (physical appearance) is cute, handsome, or sexy.

Some women are drawn to what is called the "BAD BOYS MENTALITY", men who are known to be disruptive, rebellious violent (on occasion) and even vulgar.

Knowing this does nothing to keep them away, but instead these women believe by denial that they have some magical ability that will keep them safe in this kind of relationship, this is denial on a high level.

So, what is it that makes a woman believe she can enter into a relationship such as the one described, and not be negatively affected by it? Denial.

"No ones perfect, you have to take the good with the bad." Sound familiar?

When someone is starving for attention and affection, they will often accept it anyway they can, and from anyone that can provide and satisfy that craving. And in defense of their actions we hear them say, "Don't judge me," and "It's my life not yours".

Those red flag moments happen for a reason, they are warnings, they come to keep you safe, but to ignore them is to open the door to danger as well as the possibility of death.

The door to domestic violence is not opened by force, it's opened gradually by those who often know what's being allowed in but deny what could await them.

You have to give people a chance. This is an undeniably true statement but should not be taken to mean disregard red flag facts.

Women generally speaking, have a fixer upper attitude, one of nurturing, mothering and even smothering. They somehow feel they can fix or change the man in "Their" relationship.

If somehow the woman can TRAIN their partner to be what they want them to be, their life, and everyone else's life would be fine.

Do you see the danger here? It's not a relationship but becomes ownership, which is the root of domestic and other violence.

In domestic violence it's victim and prey, the strong verses the weak. Strong by the way does not mean rebellious no more than weak means timid.

Domestic violence is about absolute power over the other person and in the course of demonstrating this power and who's boss it can become physically abusive.

Two fighters enter the ring both have the same goal in mind, and that's to win the fight. Much will depend on how prepared each person is and what kind of training they have received. So, we must look into the past and what contributed to them being brought to this point in time.

Every fighter brings something to the ring with them, and that is the experiences of previous fights, wins and losses.

Every potential relationship also brings with them

baggage as well, and it's important how this baggage is addressed moving forward.

Round 4
In This Corner

In my many years of public speaking and teaching there is a book that I have often encouraged couples, and those who were thinking about getting into a relationship to read. It's title, "Men are from Mars women are from Venus" By John Gray it's a book on, and about relationships.

This book is not the end all to building a relationship but it's a helpful tool, and aid I recommend, we will talk about it in a few moments.

Understanding, becomes difficult if the communication is not good. In most relationships I have found that those involved spend the majority of their time talking at one another, and not to one another.

To better understand this, we must take a look back before we move forward. Here's where many relationships get stalled.

There is no real time given to learning about the person they want to spend the rest of their lives with.

It's dangerous to have a "I love them just the way they are" mentality which speaks volumes to denial.

There should be extreme caution when it comes to entering and developing a relationship.

Think for a moment, when we go to purchase a car we want to know all we can about it, for the dealer to show us the car facts, miles on the vehicle, how old it is, etc…, and when we go to buy a home we seek information about who lived in it last (if not a new home), if it has old plumbing or new, does the house meet code, what the neighborhood is like and more.

Yet, when it concerns a relationship, we don't investigate anything or are quickly satisfied based on little information, and accept the relationship "AS IS." All other matters can become bothersome details.

When should we get to know the person we seek to spend our life with? Immediately is not fast enough, and even then it's not a guarantee there will not be issues to address.

Questions you should ask yourself before getting into any relationship.

1) Did you grow up in a double of single parent home?
2) How many siblings were in the home with you?
   A) Girls
   B) Boys

3) Are you the oldest child (if not where in order were you)?

4) Were there any drinkers or smokers in your home?

5) Have you ever been abused or witnessed abuse in your home?

6) Are you a smoker or drinker, and if so, how regularly, daily, weekly, monthly?

7) Have you ever hit someone when you became angry?

8) What do you like most about yourself?

9) What do you like least about yourself?

10)   If you could change one thing in your life what would it be?

To have a fight, two individuals have to agree to enter the ring to do so. To enter a relationship requires the interested parties to be willing to do so also.

Although it's not possible to know everything about another human being, it is however possible to learn a great deal about them. But before that can take place, you need to know about yourself.

The above questions were designed to help you look at yourself, as this is where you need to start to understand why you do what you do or allow certain things to take place in your life.

As I have said before, as a public speaker I have

sat with numerous individuals, some who have been victims of violence, both domestic, and otherwise.

When asked why they believe things happen to them in their relationship many of these women automatically resort to self-blaming.

Or they will finger point to the man and the things he did not, or would not do, to keep or make them happy.

Our present lives are cluttered by our past. We can't escape them, but we don't have to revive them. This is what we labeled baggage. We all come with baggage, but few of us learn how to address what we have placed inside.

One of the issues I've been faced with through the years has been women who have no desire to see or accept where they have made mistakes when it came to getting into a new relationship or even a first one.

For many women, everything in their last relationship if put on a percentage bases the man did over 90% of what was found wrong with the relationship.

Where there is a dispute, there is also a need for resolve, this fight is about who's right and who's wrong.

These fights are usually over trivial matters that have no real significance other than that of exerting power.

When it comes to boxing, the ring announcer gives a brief description of the fighters who have entered the ring. These stats tell us about the fighters and a history of their "in the ring encounters," wins and losses.

There is the possibility of being outmatched by training, experience, height, weight, and arm reach, but there are fighters that believe they are suited to be in the ring even with the odds being against them.

There are some fights that should never take place under any circumstance, and those who enter the ring are aware that someone could be injured and worst case scenario, die.

As we look at some stats included in this book it's sad to see how much violence has become the norm and almost culturally accepted.

Think about it for a moment, a man enters the ring standing 6 feet 4 inches, and weighting 289 lbs. in one corner, and in the other corner stands a woman 5 foot 2 inches, weighting 110 lbs.

Of course we know this is not going to be a fair fight, but something inside of human beings still clamor to see what will take place and few will say this is not right or acceptable as they have come to see a fight, and to see blood and brutality.

Round 5
The Challenge

What is it that makes someone turn to violence as the way to deal with differences that come in a relationship?

When it comes to any relationship there will be challenges that will come up to test that bond. But it's important to know yourself better before entering one with another individual.

Before a boxer gets into the ring for a fight they try to know all they can about their opponent. This information can come by way of a number of sources, weight, height, reach, wins and losses, why?

It's to exploit their weaknesses as many as can be taken advantage of. Fighters want to know where the chinks are in the armor where the Achilles heel is located.

When it comes to domestic violence the same is also true, it's seeking and developing the best plan of attack.

There are men who will put countless hours into learning how to intimidate and control their partner through fear, abuse and violence.

In the Ring with Heels On

There are some things unknown about an opponent, until entering the ring, and the bell sounds. It's at that time the fighters will learn who has the better skills and endure.

What is it that made this fight necessary in the first place? At the core of any fight is that little thing that boast great things, called "ego."

When it comes to ego, also known as pride, it becomes very delicate, sensitive, and even fragile when someone feel theirs is under attack.

Ego, when it is under presumed attack lashes out to defend itself and could, and most times do turn violent.

Does it matter that the offending person is a woman or child? Not to those who have very fragile egos.

When a man's so-called ego is attacked, he feels that his manhood is also under attack, and that his intelligence is on the line.

He begins to think the woman is usurping authority over him, and presenting herself as better than him, so he feels it's his duty to put her back in her place, using whatever means necessary.

The man's challenge is to do whatever he deems appropriate to bring about her submission to him.

Now consider this, if he is someone who drinks regularly and is drunk, the chances are even higher that there will be some action of control demonstrated, whether it's being loud, rude, or violent.

Of course some say they are only occasional drinkers and do so only to relax and unwind, and if the woman says the drinking is becoming an issue in their relationship, then the dice have been rolled and a challenge thrown out as to who's in charge.

No matter how you slice it ego now comes into play along with past reasoning as to what might transpire.

Now that ego has presented itself more openly, it should not come as a surprise as it has manifested itself numerous times. Remember, it is a red flag moment, one that for whatever the reason was pushed aside and not dealt with.

Many homes have been violently torn apart and devastated by drinking, sex, and drugs.

Ego is all about self. It's "I", "My", and "Me" The fighter in the ring wants to destroy his opponent to prove he is the best, and is willing to take a punch to deliver one that will bring an end to the question of who's the best and that it was only done to defend themselves.

Some women see men as broken and that it's their job or duty to fix them, and so they turn a blind eye to what they see is wrong refusing to accept it.

It's like getting into the ring with someone who is known to always cheat and play dirty to win, yet think it will somehow be different with you because they say it's in the past now.

Relationships are built around trust, not blind trust, but trust. Learn as much about the person you seek to enter into a relationship with as you can. That does not mean he should fill out a form for a background check, but close. What you are looking for is honesty from A to Z.

Bear in mind that the fight starts long before the fighters enter the ring.

Relationships are about life interaction and connectivity. The challenge is to know yourself expectations and limitations.

Let's again answer a few questions

11)   Do you believe there is a perfect relationship?

12)   Do you believe your spouse should tell you everything?

13)   Have you ever dated someone with a ego problem?

40

14) Have you ever been in a violent relationship?

15) Do you feel you can change someone else if given the time to do so?

16) Do you drink, how often and for what reason?

17) What would you do if you caught your spouse looking at another woman?

18) Is there any time a man should hit a woman?

19) How do you define love?

20) If you could change anything about your life what would it be?

Now let's move from questions to some additional concerns.

Human history shows us that competition is part of our desired makeup, some have gone as far as to say it's in our DNA.

Competition is taught and so it can also be resisted as well. Everything in life is not about competition, or who's the best.

Both fighters feel they have something to prove when they climb inside the ring and that's whose in charge.

Unlike boxers there is no need to get into a relationship ring to prove who is better.

It's hard to convince some women not to take the challenge of getting into a toxic relationship. As far as they are concerned, you, the bystander, or friend, is only attempting to interrupt their chance at happiness. Many women have exchanged facts for feeling.

I have had the pleasure of counseling many individuals that were considering marriage and was asked many questions about relationships. Like a referee it was my duty to tell them what they should watch out for as well as what to avoid doing.

I'd ask if they understood what I was saying and the advise being given, and of course the response would be yes, but for many only until they walked away.

Advise is like medicine, it's only effective and help if it's taken.

The fighters challenge is to taunt their opponent before the fight begins, this is the attempt to tear down their defenses mentally and emotionally, and if done correctly the fight should not take long.

We have often been told to pick your battles and to think before we act. It's imperative to step back and take a good look before you leap and make a decision that can change your life, and affect the lives of everyone around you.

Your personal challenge is to examine carefully what it is you desire to do, and determine what is the driving force behind your action.

Honestly evaluate your thought process and proceed with caution as pride can lead you to do things that are not beneficial to your safety and those around you.

Thoughts can be deceiving and misleading where emotion is concerned. And yes, all things might be possible but are all things necessary?

Round 6
The Fear

No matter who you are, there is some aspect of fear in your life. Fear is seen as, or thought of as, a negative thing, a feeling or an emotion. But there is what I call a "healthy fear".

It's not a fear that causes panic or reduces you to being a coward, the fear I'm talking about is one of respect. I will explain this in more detail in a moment.

We have been taught that fear means **F**alse **E**vidence **A**ppearing **R**eal, and that we should have no fear of anything or anyone.

To have this type of mindset is to not respect life.

Fear is also concern, awe, fright, and even reverence. We have been taught to see fear in only one light, as that is something to avoid and run away from and is harmful.

Fear is seen as darkness and evil, and although this definition can be true, this is not always the case.

We will look at both aspects of fear in this chapter the darkness of it as well as light.

One type of fear can render you powerless, the other can make you powerful, once you understand the role they both can play in your life.

Fear as it applies to our subject, In the Ring with Heels on, we will be talking primarily about the violent and abusive fear.

Fear must be instilled to be effective, and this installation comes most often by way of intimidation.

A fighter (or abuser) must present themselves as bigger, stronger and more fierce than their opponent. Their statistics most often speaks for them in the wins to loss ratio.

One of the greatest tools of an abuser is that of fear. Let's look at some overall stats for athletes and domestic violence before we continue.

Be mindful that we now live in a culture that promotes violence, meaning there is not much in the way of consequences for the use of it.

Women are seen to be, or considered lower class people when It comes to how they are treated when it comes to domestic or other violence.

Ray Rice for example, a professional Football player is seen on tape in 2014 knocking his then fiancé out in an elevator.

NFL commissioner Roger Goodell created new rules for players who abuse a partner, and up to then there was nothing in place for a players action when it came to domestic violence. The first offense they said would lead to a six-game suspension without pay and a second offense would lead to being kicked out of the league for at least a year. This however does nothing to stop domestic violence, and it gave a diminutive fine when compared to their income for violence towards a woman.

There was a survey at that time of 252 nationally-reported criminal cases in one year, that involved athletes and that report found that about 14% of the athletes involved in domestic violence were professional football players.

A contributing factor to domestic violence among football players was said to be that they had become desensitized to physical conduct (abuse), because it was part of what they did all the time.

Justifying abuse, or giving a fine for acts of physical abuse does not make it right or acceptable. And does nothing to make it go away.

Compare this to about 7% of professional baseball players, and about 6% of professional basketball and hockey players also being abusive.

While this does not draw any specific causation of their violence, the survey is at least suggesting that professional athletes who play other sports besides football also break the law in significant numbers through domestic violence.

Boxers are not exempt from this practice of violence against women. Again another sport that makes it's money based on violence towards another individual.

Boxing is known to be brutal, and can be bloody, and at it's core, it is to hurt the opponent, so they would not answer the bell.

There are boxers that have hit and abused their wives as a show of power over them and to see them as nothing more than property.

Candi Holyfield, wife of Evander Holyfield said in the protective order, that she suffered abuse, beginning about six months after they were married July 1, 2003, and again when she was pregnant with their first child. Candi said, at first it was "mainly emotional" abuse, but physical incidents had escalated beginning in 2008.

She claimed her husband choked her in front of their daughter and housekeeper in 2008, and that last year, he hit and grabbed her in front of their children. A few weeks ago, she said, he threw a bottle of water at her. But as many women that are abused do, she began to recant her statements, and cover for the abuser and his abuse.

In a statement released by the publicist, Candi Holyfield said there were "misunderstandings about what really took place and in the representation of what happened in the situation between her and her husband" but did not elaborate. (Again women tend to recant their statements for fear).

"Out of respect for our family, I ask that the media please respect our privacy," she said in the statement. "This is a private matter and your consideration of this would be much appreciated." Many acts of abuse and violence are forgiven but they are not forgotten.

Abused women are willing to take the blame, and live with the shame of abuse, rather than tell the truth about it, thinking they are causing hurt to the one that is abusing them, and numerous women believe this is a show of love for that individual.

Another example is Josie Harris, Floyd Mayweather's former long-time partner and mother to three of his four children, but she doesn't see Mayweather much anymore.

Occasionally he would collect their children in person she said, but more often than not they are transported using the jet service he uses for much of his travel outside of Las Vegas.

It's an arrangement Josie said she is happy with,

saying, It meant she didn't have to take a Xanax before he showed up.

Josie Harris told USA TODAY Sports in an interview from her home some 50 miles northwest of Los Angeles. "For some reason I still get anxiety when I know that he (Floyd) is on his way.

I have no idea why, but I get really overwhelmed (fearful) when I know that I have to be around him."

This is typical for stress that accompanies women who have been abused, when they have to deal with on a regular basis the individual who had abused them in the past.

Harris says she suffered physical abuse from the boxer on "six occasions," the worst took place she said in September 2010, when Mayweather entered Harris' home while she slept, yanked her to the floor by her hair, then punched and kicked and screamed cuss words at her, all this done in front of their children.

Abusers, (famous or not), don't consider their effect on anyone else they are only focused on themselves.

It was the couple's oldest son, Koraun, who slipped out of the house to alert a security guard to call the police.

Mayweather was eventually sentenced to 90 days in prison. This was one of seven alleged assaults Mayweather had committed against five different women that resulted in his being arrested or issued a citation. Sadly, it's been proven that citations, and restraining orders do nothing to stop abuse.

Floyd's former fiancée, Shantel Jackson, filed a civil lawsuit against him including claims of battery, false imprisonment and the allegations that the fighter pointed a gun at her.

Fear and intimidation often prevents a woman from reporting, and following up with legal actions, to possibly prevent additional abuse.

Some women are scared off, while others are paid off, to remain quiet, many are not willing to have their name in the news or public domain.

If the ego driven man can get the woman to get in the emotional ring, it would be by her choice he would say, and therefore what happens is because of her and would come by her own doing even physical violence.

A boxer, (abuser) feels they can justify their action by simply stating that, she got in the ring with them, and therefore she should be treated as anyone else getting in the ring.

In the mouth, and mind of the abuser there is

always an excuse prepared for their action.

Even sadder is when a woman accepts the blame for the violence against her or her children, why?

Usually, what takes place in the abused individuals life is based on what has taken place in their past, what they have been exposed to, and what they accept as an accepted course of action to take, based on previous experiences.

What we are taught has an effect on us and can influence us in a positive or negative way.

What tends to go through an individual's mind is not known until there are actions of the subconscious brought into the consciousness.

I spoke earlier of fear and that it can be positive, this fear is a "healthy fear", an empowering not a cowering fear.

This particular fear I speak of here, is a reverential fear, one of respect, and many women believe this to be the fear they use in their relationship, even when they have been abused.

You hear them defend the abuser saying how much they love the person who has harmed them, saying it was not all his fault, even cover for them, and believing they should stand by their man as a show of solidarity and support.

It's unfortunate that we have been led to believe things without investigating them. To understand others is to first understand ourselves.

Round 7

Ready to Rumble

The fighters are in the ring, friends and family, sponsors and spectators are in attendance, everyone is waiting to see what will happen next.

When a relationship begins, everyone is curious to know what will take place, and if the relationship will gather steam or fizzle.

There are people that support both sides of a fight, some even saying, this not an even match-up, but will sit and watch to see what will happen. Some hoping for success, others looking for failure, and something to critique or condemn, even hoping to say I TOLD YOU SO.

This has a similar feel to what takes place when there is domestic violence.

The ring announcer stands prepared to make their call, as the fighters are given their instructions in the middle of the ring by the referee.

Each fighter stoically looking the other in the eyes, both having the same goal in mind and that is to win.

What is it that brought these two people into the ring in the first place?

We have spoken about relationships, but it's this very word that has confused many women and men alike.

Those being abused often seek to enter a positive relationship, often having no idea what a real relationship is, and they base their choice on what they have experienced in the past, and hoping to have learned a valuable life lesson and not repeating or bringing negative issues to it.

Their relationship perception is slanted, because they saw very little positive action taking place in their home lives by parents. So violence, and abuse in the home was often injected into those living and subjected to those abusive conditions.

This by no means is to say every child has to become abusive or violent because they have been exposed to it. But the chances are greater for them to do so because of it.

Some individuals learned to take a negative and turn it into a positive by making healthy choices.

With that said let's look at what might have taken place outside the ring leading up to the fight.

In all the years of my teaching, and counseling I have never had one person come to me saying they had entered a violent, or abusive relationship that began on day one, even those who had seen the potential of it looming.

In the courting, or dating phase, couples usually put on their best behavior, it's the wine and dine stage, the days and nights of sweet-talking cuddling and often sex.

In this phase the woman sees everything she hopes for and dreamed of, she by her feelings and appearance seemed to have found her knight, her man in shining armor and the future father of her babies.

She has waited and finally found the man who made her heart skip a beat, her SOUL MATE. At last all is right with the world.

Women who are so focused on their "WANT FOR A MAN" and need a man list, that they are willing to ignore red flag moments when they appear, and become disappointed when the reality of who they are truly with surfaces.

Human nature is to love, and be loved, we don't often understand love, but we seek it, and many women because they are the individuals that carry another human life inside them usually have very nurturing spirits.

Men and women are different for a reason, it's called balance, what one can do that the other cannot is what gives this balance.

These differences should not be exploited, but explored, and developed, they are not weaknesses but strengths.

Women see things differently from men and men see things differently than women.

This does not mean one is right and the other is wrong, or that one is superior to the other.

Sometimes it's possible to be saying the same thing but unable to communicate it properly, and because this is true, it has led to verbal confrontations that can, and in some instances, do, lead to physically abusive behavior by some men.

Looking for love, or what is thought to be love in all the wrong places (or men), has done its fair share of damage in relationships.

When in the dating phase, rose colored glasses

are worn, it's the "wow" moments of there's no one like him. It's blinding self to little warning signs in behavior or conversation.

But this is how emotional deception operates. I have spoken to women who thought they had it together, knew what they wanted to do in life, and were in pursuit of their dreams, but abruptly canceled these dreams for what they thought was a dream relationship.

Some women would attempt to mask their hurt and pain rather than to deal with it, so they cover up one bad relationship with another, and justifying it by saying to themselves again, "This is the one".
When someone wants to be loved they will settle for whatever gets them to FEEL they are loved.

It's what we have been taught about attention, "even negative attention is better than no attention".

There was a young lady, Ann (*not her real name*) I spent a brief time with counseling her and she was in a relationship that was not positive and she wanted to know what she should do to make him (her boyfriend) happy?

This is where many women are when it comes to relationships, they seek to do what they believe will please a man, and push their own lives into a corner as not being important.

Ann was willing to let her life and her dreams fade if she could acquire them by what she could do for her man. In other words she thought pleasing him would get her what she wanted from life.

I asked Ann about herself and what was her goal in life? Her response, to get married and have a family, live in a nice home and drive a new car.

With Ann, and so many other women they seek the happily ever after scenario. Ann, in the dating phase thought the world of Todd (*not his actual name*), it seemed his eyes were on her, and life was about her only. Then a few months into their relationship things began to change.

Ann felt Todd was not giving her all his attention, they were not going out as much, and he was coming home later than usual.

Ann could see her hopes and dreams of family being dashed, and she needed to confront Todd, who promptly shoved her and swore at her. She said that was the beginning of the times he would put his hands on her, and each time it became worse, and even leading to her being beat unconscious on the street in front of witnesses.

Why did Todd feel he had to take such an action against Ann, the person he had entered into a relationship with? The amazing thing here is they were both on an emotional collision course with one another because they lacked the knowledge of what a relationship really involved.

Percent of women reporting intimate partner and non-partner violence

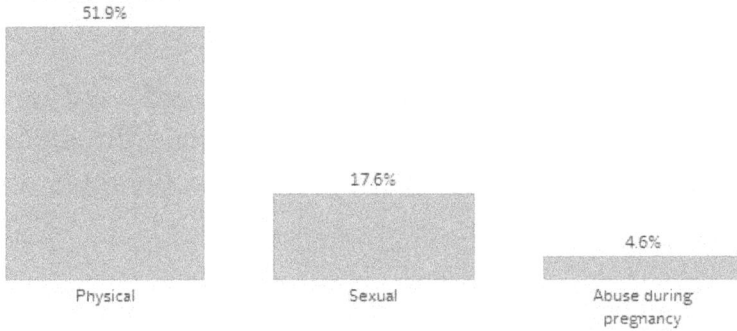

Source: UN Women

Todd's back story and history was that of a broken home, and broken promises. He came from a home where the man was king, and a woman was never to question him. Todd had seen his father control the home, and his father was not above using violence to make his point clear.

Todd was raised believing a woman should know her place, and stay in it, and if she did not, you did what you had to do to get her to comply.

In the dating phase of Ann and Todd's relationship, there was no problem, because she was accepting of what he would do, that changed the moment she began questioning him. To Todd she began to see herself as an equal, and he was taught the opposite.

Now it's time to learn who's the boss. Ann has entered the ring against Todd, now it's time to fight.

40 to 60 Percent of men who abuse women also abuse their children.

The number of teenage girls who said they have been in a relationship where the boyfriend threatened violence, or self-harm if they were to breakup was said to be 1 in 5.

The percentage of domestic violence victims who are women is said to be about 85%.

EVERY 9 SECONDS A WOMAN IS ABUSED IN THE UNITED STATES

Consider the following. The number of workdays American employees miss each year because of domestic violence is said to be about 175,000. A staggering number of lost days of wages.

The highest percentage of female murder victims is said to be 40 to 70 percent in the U.S.

Women who were killed by their husbands or boyfriends, often it's within an ongoing abusive relationship that started out with what seemed to be a partnership.

The ring announcer lets everyone know it's time for the fight to begin, sides have been chosen, who will come out on top, but the bigger question is why is this fight even necessary in the first place?

Many have asked this question, but found the answer is never clear. Most not having a clue as to how they arrived at this point in their lives, wondering what happened to the person they met and who seemed to love them so much.

The relationship now requires a referee, a middle person to oversee what is about to take place, that for all practical purposes could have possibly been avoided.

So far not one blow has been exchanged but the fight is about to begin, and all that is required now, is the trigger, the sound of the bell.

With domestic and other violence there is always a trigger, and it differs from individual to individual, and what these triggers might be we will explore as we move forward. **Getting ready does not mean you are prepared for what might follow**.

Taking a Punch

When the bell sounds, the combatants meet in the center ring, and the real fight begins, it is very serious, and often turns very ugly quickly.

The fights that take place at home behind closed doors don't have referees. The bell ringer, is found to be the individual on the other end of a 911 call.

To Begin with, is there any reason why a man feels he has to become physical with a woman, his wife, or his girlfriend?

Let's look at one possibility. This does not justify being physically abusive, although some make the attempt to do so.

Relationships for some is not about companionship, but it's seen as one person becoming another person's exclusive property.

Of course, the men who feel they are justified in their reason for striking a woman will often say, it's something the woman brought on themselves, as a consequence for some action they took, or was unwilling to take in order to please the man.

Violence is driven by, and based on strong, but negative emotions. We are told and asked to believe these are crimes of passion, performed by individuals who were simply not thinking straight.

Physical violence has become acceptable and even profitable as seen in how much money is made from selling tickets to be a witness to hurt being inflicted on another human being.

With violence all around us there is no wonder why it's also managed to become part of the behavior we find in our homes as well.

> WOMEN WHO ARE VICTIMS
> OF DOMESTIC VIOLENCE
> ARE EIGHT TIMES MORE LIKELY
> TO BE KILLED BY AN INTIMATE
> PARTNER IF THERE ARE
> FIREARMS IN THE HOME.

Once the fighters leave their corner, they have but one main thought, to dominate, to exercise immediate control over their opponent, to bring the pain, and finally end the fight quickly controlling the outcome.

All fights are not the same and the expected outcome may not be what was anticipated if the other fighter can take a punch, if they can take the abuse.

With domestic violence taking a punch becomes one of those family secrets rarely if ever spoken about.

Violence is not something that just happens, it's something that is triggered through association, as to what that trigger might be is known only to the individual that housed it.

To justify abuse, you have to make it acceptable. This is done easy enough since it's promoted all around us and daily by way of all media outlets.

Over the years I've sat across the table from couples who were in toxic relationships and more times than I would like to recount there have been women who felt they were trapped in a situation they could not see themselves free from.

Part of the reason for this is their partner had spent time working on their self-esteem and self-worth, and one of the keys to this power is to isolate them from family and friends.

This is done with subtlety, often lavishing material things on them and finding what makes them tick physically and emotionally and supplying them with what they feel they were missing.

It was about giving them a false sense of security and once they are comfortable, the abuser slowly begin to pull the cover off who they really were all along.

There are men who have no problem with hitting women if this is what they believe is the best way to control them.

Unlike the boxers inside the square circle there is no one to stand between these fighters and even if there were, chances are good they will be injured in the process as those prong to violence do not consider who they hurt as long as they achieve their goal.

Where there is no respect there can be found the willingness to cause bodily harm to another human being. Some abuse has led to death.

Consider the following fact. **The number of American troops killed in Afghanistan and Iraq between 2001 and 2012 was 6,488.**

The number of American women who were murdered by current or ex male partners during that same time was 11,766. This is almost double.

There was an outcry nationally for those in uniforms overseas and barely a whimper for the women who died at the hands of their partners.

Fighters entering the ring has what is known as the Marcus of Queensberry rules.

These are Guidelines or instructions for fighters to follow in the ring supposedly for their safety.

It was not uncommon to find fighters cheating in order to gain a victory.

What is a person willing to do to win, to have power over another, and to have status? For some, whatever it takes.

With the home becoming the boxing rings of today there are rules or laws that have been put in place that were designed to help women who have been abused, they are restraining orders, and orders of protection that so far has not been worth the paper they are written on.

Women are afraid to seek them because they fear it will enrage their ex-partners even more to seek to do them harm.

No home should be a boxing ring where everything is done based on threats, intimidation and abuse. The 9 second rule applies here, every 9 seconds a woman is being abused, it could be on her job, in a car or at home.

Some would ask why would a woman enter a fight she could not possibly win, and why would she even think to get in the ring at all?

First, I don't want you to think only in terms of a physical ring. We are speaking metaphorically, in the hope of painting a clear picture of what is being done to the women of our nation, and around the world.

Some of the greatest dangers is not outside, but inside the home. When it comes to abuse it does not begin with physical violence. Most begins emotionally as the introduction to other abuse.

THE FIRST PUNCH is done emotionally and psychologically. It's a mental attack. Abusers like to get into their victim's head as we have spoken about in the chapter hype. The verbal fight is what leads up to the physical confrontation, it's what has been called the fight before the fight.

These verbal fight matches are usually blow for blow word altercations that seen harmless enough but lead to dangerous conditions of control.

These arguments are most often associated with drinking, alcohol, drugs, or media.

The fight bell rings often as the struggle for power or dominance ensues.

What is it the sets the abuser off, it could be as simple as questioning what they do or have done in the past?

The first punch hurts emotionally. For instance, the abuser might begin with calling the woman a "STUPIT B---H", for noncompliance, or that he would "KICK HER A--", if she continued to question what he does, or not leave him alone.

Alcohol, drugs, jealousy and finances are most often the catalyst behind domestic violence. Hidden beneath them is disrespect as each of them gives a distorted perception of respect.

Alcohol emboldens individuals giving them the power to say what they really think, or as some have said, "speak their sober mind". Drugs rewire the mental capacity, often bringing about what I call **"The Superman Affect"** thinking they are invincible and can do no wrong.

Men overall have been taught to believe they are the KING OF THEIR CASTLE and never to be questioned, but the problem isn't the castle it's PRIDE.

If there is a swing and a miss, verbally, then the stakes need to be raised. The abuser then feels he has to prove something, that he is the best, and that he is number one always.

Violence begins internally and become visible when the individual does not get what they want, and what is that, absolute control?

Men with fragile egos are quick to turn to violence as a way to make their point clear. These are men who are emotionally weak and will use violence as a way to demonstrate they are strong and that they will not be opposed by anyone for any reason at anytime. So they begin with a flurry of emotional punches and should they land psychologically, he feels he now has the advantage in the ring.

But if the emotional abuse does not get the expected result then it's time to move to the next level of control.

Round 9
You Hit Like a Girl

There is the punch before the punch as we have seen in the last chapter. It's the emotional punch that is thrown with the purpose of disarming and unsettling the other individual. How effective this is depends on the abusers ability to intimidate, first without violence, but it's in their mind to use it should it become necessary, and for abusers they feel it always becomes necessary.

Violence begins with testing the water, it's moving to predator and prey, its going from pushing to punching, and from having fits, to throwing fist.

Culturally we are brainwashed to believe certain aspects about the sexes such as, men are to be the bread winners, and the woman is the homemaker, and baby maker.

As a child I grew up hearing things like "little girls are made from sugar and spice and all that is nice", and little boys are made from snaps and snails and puppy dogs tails", that "men are superior and women are inferior" and a woman can never be equal to a man.

Women and men are inherently different from one another, this goes without saying, and I must say that

I appreciate the differences, but not everyone feels the same way.

In the world of boxing, a transformation has taken place as it comes to women. Many women now feel they are qualified to step in the square circle, that they can prove they are just as good as any man stepping in the ring.

I spoke about Muhammad Ali earlier, one of the best-known fighters of all time.

He had 9 children possibly 10. One of these children was Laila Ali, born December 30th, 1977, who had her first pro boxing match in October of 1999. When she told her father her plans to box, she said he was not happy with her decision.

Boxing is dangerous, as it is more about inflicting damage to the opponent's upper body but mainly focusing on their head for a knockout.

Boxing is one of the most violent and brutal so-called sports, and sadly it's brutality is what people are willing to pay for and see.

Is there any wonder why people are filled with rage and pinned up hostility towards others, festering and boiling inside waiting on a release, often finding it in acts of aggression towards others including loved ones.

We've been taught to look at everything through eyes of competition, who's the best, winners' verses losers, first and last, superior and inferior. This mentality is carried into almost every aspect of our lives including our relationships.

Violence and abusive behavior follow cycles that can be clearly seen.

There is a common thread between women and men, and that is emotions and feelings. How we feel, and our attitudes often determine our course of action.

Emotions lead actions. It's taking things to the next level when threats and intimidation get no result.

There are certain formulas that can be found in the lives of domestic violent abusers, and we list a few of them on the next page of examples. **There are cycles of abuse**.

The abuse begins with the first hit, and it doesn't matter if it's physical or mental, and once initiated it becomes easy for the abuser to justify, or continue to justify their action.

Domestic violence is a mentality that can be traced back to a beginning and origin source, and has a history of influence.

Look carefully at the process and progress that accompany domestic violence.

A boxer doesn't just go to the ring and say they wish to fight. There are issues and events in their life that leads them to this point of punishment. These influences were determining factors for fighting.

A man does not suddenly hit and abuse a woman, there is something that triggered this action. For many of us this is the "why, mystery".

We can track the history and influences of why an individual wants to get into a ring and decides to fight in the first place, the why becomes clear.

Why, requires investigation, something not given much time as we are living in a hurried and reactive society.

With such a rise in domestic violence it's become clear that we need to be more proactive, and take the time to examine cause and effect.

On the accompanying chart you can begin to see how domestic abusers have a cycle and pattern of behavior.

Circle and Cycle of Violence

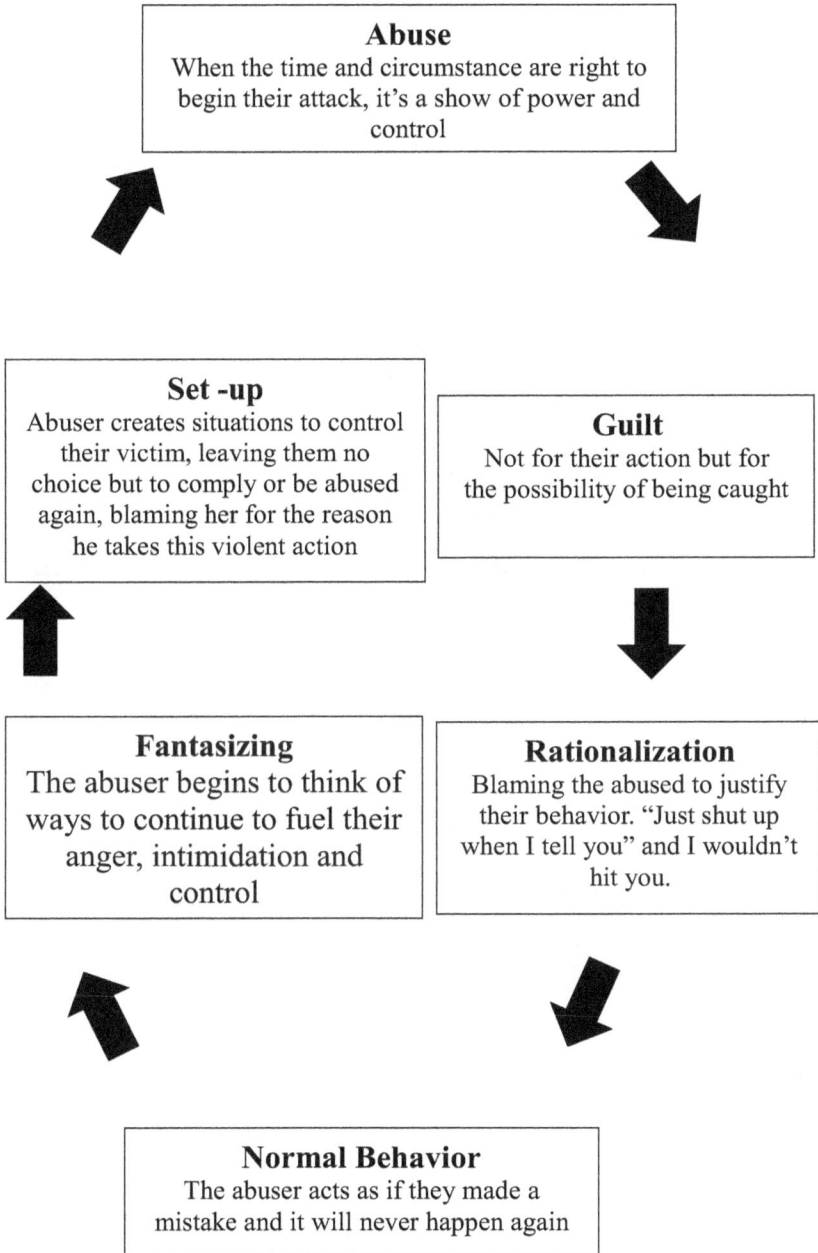

Abuse
When the time and circumstance are right to begin their attack, it's a show of power and control

Set -up
Abuser creates situations to control their victim, leaving them no choice but to comply or be abused again, blaming her for the reason he takes this violent action

Guilt
Not for their action but for the possibility of being caught

Fantasizing
The abuser begins to think of ways to continue to fuel their anger, intimidation and control

Rationalization
Blaming the abused to justify their behavior. "Just shut up when I tell you" and I wouldn't hit you.

Normal Behavior
The abuser acts as if they made a mistake and it will never happen again

Is there some way a woman can know with any degree of certainty what a man might be capable of doing? There are signs that she should pay close attention to.

These are again RED FLAG MOMENTS.

Some would like to believe there is no way to know what anyone might or might not do. The key to being successful in any relationship begins with **SELF SAFETY**, and **this should always remain high on your priority list of concerns**.

 What many women fear is listening to their inner voice that seeks to keep them safe, even overriding that voice, often for a false feeling of companionship, and easing loneliness.

Women must not have a "anything for a man mentality", this is often where their sorrows begin.

In the years I have spoken to women this is where many of them go wrong. No one thinks when they enter a relationship that it might become physical, but it's important that women look carefully at the things a potential relationship partner has done in their past, as well as how they communicate, and interact with family members.

Look at the cycle.

1-Abuse is not random, it's often planned, and

the abuser merely waits for what they consider the right time to attack. It's like the lion hunting their prey, everything must be right, or the intended target will get away.

Fact: Three women a day are murdered by partners, and over 38 million women have been already abused in their lifetime.

Over 4.7 million women suffer from being abused every year.

What's also sad is the number of children that have witnessed their parents being abused, it's estimated to be over 8,000,000,00 and counting.

Hitting and fighting is done with the intent to hurt, and cause harm, it's to make a point, and clearly let the opponent know who's in charge.

The natural response to being struck is to protect one's self, and become defensive, and even to strike back, leading to additional attacks or abuse.

2- Guilt. Some men will show momentary guilt, not for their actions but for the possibility of being caught, or reprimanded, or possibly arrested for their action.

3-Rationalization. Abusers are prepared to justify what they did and do, it's blaming the violence on the victim, often saying they made them hit them, and everything could have been avoided had she just kept her mouth shut, she was attacked because she was embarrassing him, and she had to be taught a lesson of who is in control.

4-Normal behavior. Abusers will sometimes normalize their actions by false apologies saying, it was a onetime mistake, and poor judgment, and it will never happen again.

In the boxing world, it's taking a cheap shot, and hitting below the belt, and hoping not to be caught.

5-Fantasizing. Those who have acted out their violent intent have thought of how they would not be opposed to taking even more drastic action if needed. Some abusers even fantasized taking deadly actions if pushed to do so.

6-Set-up. Abusers will set-up situations that they have complete control over the outcome by use of fear and intimidation, even causing the woman to fail a command, to give them a reason to hit them.

The goal is to make the woman strike out at them physically, so they can say they were only defending themselves.

I've instructed and encouraged women over the years to take time to investigate the individuals they plan to spend time with.

Many of us will not eat certain foods until we know what's in it. If you are particular about the clothes you buy, the nail polish you will wear, and how you look, you should be just as careful about who you will allow in your life as a relationship partner.

But when it comes to relationships, we often accept sight unseen, and not investigate the words that come out of their mouths and the actions that support them.

ON A TYPICAL DAY,
THERE ARE MORE THAN

20,000 PHONE CALLS

PLACED TO DOMESTIC
VIOLENCE HOTLINES

People are worth more than property, so don't ignore the red flag warning signs that are built in. Please don't hesitate to make a call and do what you have to for yours, or your own family's safety.

Round 10
When is Enough, Enough?

When a fighter enters a ring the desired outcome is a KO (knock out) or even a TKO (Technical knockout) and the sooner the better. When a fight takes too long it becomes a question of skill. In the eyes of the onlooker it means one fighter is not as good as they said they were.

Fighting, particularly violent fighting is about proving ones superiority over another person.

Domestic violence is senseless violence against a woman.

Black women experience domestic violence at a rate that is 35% higher than white women

Domestic violence has nothing to do with love, whether real or imagined. Love is not shown through brutality, but through gentleness and kindness.

Physical abuse is not an accident, it's done purposely and intentionally. A black eye, a busted lip and cracked ribs is not a sign of love in any sense of the word.

So, when is enough enough? When does a woman come to the place in her life that she has taken all she could from an abusive partner?

Maybe we can help answer these questions, but first, let's take some time and look at a few women who survived domestic violence.

Ava's story. I was 18 when we first met. He was nearly 10 years older and at first I didn't like him (**Red Flag moment**), but I eventually agreed to go out with him. And quite typically, he was kind, attentive and friendly, and I soon fell for him. I keep thinking if I just stopped and looked, **I would've seen the signs and could have ran away** before it got to the point of being too scared to even leave the house. But of course, hindsight is a wonderful thing, and all I saw was a good looking, sweet and loving man, whom I was lucky to be dating. (*It's dangerous when you ignore the insight and foresight*).

Things moved pretty fast, I remember him telling me he loved me after a few weeks, he told me how wonderful and amazing I was (*The predator was circling his prey*). He used to pick me up in his car and drive me anywhere I wanted; if I called he'd always answer like he was so happy to talk to me.

I don't know exactly when it started going wrong, but it was soon into the relationship. He'd tell me that he didn't like me talking to other men, and 'that's just how he is', he'd leer at other women in front of me, and tell me how attractive they were, and how women would ask him out all the time, if I got upset he'd shout at me and tell me I had to deal with it, and if I ever did it to him, he'd leave me.

This soon progressed, his behavior got more and more controlling and jealous, he wouldn't let me out the house unless he knew about it, and if I did leave he'd call me constantly asking me when I'd get home. I wasn't allowed to wear clothes he didn't like, even when I wore a t-shirt and jeans he's tell me I looked tarty.

He'd stop me getting any job, unless it was with him, I wasn't allowed to talk to any man, or even if I looked at one, he'd scream at me until I walked with my head down.

I wasn't allowed to see my family, or friends without constant questions, so in the end, I thought why bother? I couldn't even order food, because he didn't trust me with the delivery man.

Things were about to move from verbal abuse to physical abuse.

I still remember the first time he hit me. I previously told him if he ever hit me I'd be gone (*very few women follow up with action*). He must have waited until I was further under his control to lay his hands on me.

We had been together a year when it happened, I was late getting home because the taxi was late, and I knew as soon as he told me to come outside and into his car there would be trouble and further abuse. As soon as I got in, he grabbed me by the neck and screamed at me for being late, he then locked the car and drove like a lunatic while grabbing and choking me. I left him that night even though he cried and told me how sorry he was, and that it would never ever happen again. I felt so sorry for him and forgave him. *And as often happens she went back to him*)

This went on for years, he didn't usually have to hit me, he had enough control over me already, if I was talking all he had to do was give me a look and I knew I had to shut up. I was scared every morning of what he would do that day. I had a panic attack when he was shouting at me one day, because I was just too emotionally tired at being accused of lying and cheating. I couldn't handle it anymore. I felt sick, I believed him when he told me, **if I just behaved, he wouldn't have to do this**.

Ava placed blame on herself thinking that all she had to do was more to please him, and things would be fine.

I thought if I showed him I could be trusted, and I loved him he'd get better, he'd love me enough to stop, he had to surely? But these things go in cycles, just as I thought he'd improved 'something' (my fault, naturally) would happen and I'd be at square one again.

He never hit me too hard (*she began to justify his actions*), it was usually pushes, grabbing my arm, choking me or slapping me. Once the neighbors heard my screams, and called the police while he was choking me, I remember not being able to breathe, and thinking I might die. As soon as the doorbell rang, he stopped, and suddenly looked calm and under control, he told me not to tell the police he hit me, and I did as I was told. (*method of fear and intimidation*)

Of course, no one knew about the abuse, he was so careful not to mark my face, and to everyone who knew him, he was the kindest, gentlest man.

Only behind closed doors was he this monster who raged at me, if my eyes have even looked at another man's. The worst part was he'd trick me into believing he'd really changed, of course he's play the **'I'm so sorry'** card many times, and I felt so guilty, and loved him so much, I instantly forgave him, but it was how he'd tell me I could dress how I please, and I thought he'd really changed this time, there was hope, and suddenly he'd tell me how tarty and horrible I looked and I wasn't to dress like this anymore.

There were times when I wanted to die just to get away, I felt confused, angry, hurt and emotionally exhausted, all from the man claiming to love me.

I was scared for my life, and believed him when he told me he'd kill me if I ever left, but I also knew I couldn't live my life like this, as I'd either kill myself, or he'd kill me.

You cannot change anyone other than yourself. So, I read. I educated myself on domestic violence and forced myself into believing it wasn't my fault, and he would never get better.

I also kept a diary of every time he hit me, or verbally abused me, so I couldn't tell myself it never happened, or let him convince me it wasn't that bad. It took another year to finally leave him.

Even though I stayed in this abusive relationship for years, and stayed with a man who treated me worse than anyone ever could, I am very proud of myself for finally leaving, no matter how long it took.

Anyone going through this, or have been through this kind of abuse knows that domestic violence wears you down, it kills your self-esteem, and you literally feel you are trapped, and that there's no way out.

Ava's story is not new or unusual. I'm sure almost every woman suffering from, or survived being abused can identify with Ava.

But like Ava there has to come a time when a woman says to herself enough is enough. That they will no longer allow themselves to be a punching bag for an abusive partner.

Let's look at another story that of Cherise.

It was Saturday night. Saturday's were always our night to party, this Saturday was no different. We'd get up and do household chores and then get together to go shopping because we had to buy something new every so often just to keep our wardrobe fresh.

This particular Saturday was different, as Cherise and I walked into a local shoe store where we were stopped by a childhood friend of Marquis.

I had known Marquis since I was in the third grade he was my second friend that I had acquired at the new school I attended.

Of course he was inquiring about my best friend Cherise. I had met her a few years prior to this day because she worked with my mom and as usual my mom always took some young lady under her wing. My mom introduced her to me as my new sister, and I treated her accordingly ever since.

Cherise and I became attached at the hip. She was pretty, a petite frame of about 4'11 with heels on. Beautiful caramel skin and eyelashes so long and pretty people pay to get them. Marquis had spotted her that day, and of course you could guess that he stopped me to find out who she was.

I told him he knows my rule on my friends dating each other, so I wasn't going to be playing match maker, but if he wanted to talk to her he had to do it himself. To my surprise he approached her himself, and with his looks and charm she became very interested in him as well.

Cherise had many questions as we rode home, and I told her everything I could remember, Marquis and I had only been friends for about 12 years at the time. I told her of our friendship, but I had never really witnessed him in a relationship to know what he was like.

I told her of our wild stories of fighting, and drugs, of him being protective of me and him being one of the people that taught me the streets and how to fight.

He had always run the neighborhood, and was well known, but she wasn't from my neighborhood, Cherise was a heights girl. They were completely from two separate worlds, but I feel like that was the thing that had pulled them together. He was the bad boy, she was the good girl. So the story goes that opposites attract. She was fresh out of a relationship where we had both just had babies. The relationship with her daughters' father had been dramatic, and heartbreaking to say the least.

So this new relationship was like a breath of fresh air for her. Marquis was attentive and sweet. Tentative and caring. Loving and understanding, she was in such a different place after the breakup with her daughters' father that all I could do was be happy for her.

They were going on dates, watching movies and having great conversation. I hadn't seen her smile like that the whole first year or so of our friendship. We had planned pregnancies with my second child and her first one. We had read two books on how to be a sexy man and a sexy woman. In following those steps we had both become pregnant. Although we had gotten pregnant it didn't bring either of us joy in our relationship, but we were happy about the pregnancy.

Now that she was over the break up with her daughters father, and was in a better place with a man that was perfect in her mind. Life couldn't be better. She was developing a great friendship and it was good for all of us. I could be around both my friends when I wanted to kick it and she wasn't missing out on her relationship time.

Then one day things changed for me. We decided that we wanted to play a game of spades (*something we always did*), and I needed a partner. It was my best friend Cherise, her boyfriend/my childhood Marquis, myself and my mother.

We went to my mother's house it was a great in between home and she knew all parties. As we sat in my mothers living room playing cards a small argument started between them. Nothing big, a card game can get intense when you are losing, or get set in a game of spades, because your partner didn't read your playing style.

My Mom and I we had been playing cards for years together so it was a very competitive game for all of us. On one particular hand they were set, and my mother and I were laughing because we had been talking big trash during that hand.

Cherise made a comment saying, that was stupid, why did you play that card last, why didn't you play that on one of the other spades. He started yelling that he wasn't stupid. Now the confusion had begun, and we saw another side of Marquis. Cherise said "That Was Stupid" not that he was stupid, but in his mind that is what he had heard, so he began yelling at her.

When she yelled back, he threw his cards across the table, cards hitting her, my mother, and myself.

This brought us all to our feet. At that time, he lunged passed me and my mother, and physically attacked her, tackling her to the floor, and started to choke her.

The actions that followed cause my mother to grab her pistol and escort him out of the house. I couldn't believe what I had seen, I had never seen him put his hands on a female before.

Cherise was shook up but no major injuries and after he calmed down he was apologetic and even cried. Little did we know that was only the beginning of what he would do. We would hear of arguments but never anything physical.

Then there was an incident where she left, went to the store directly across the street from her apartment leaving her daughter with Marquis, and came back she went to check on her daughter and she wasn't breathing.

She took the baby to the emergency room, where they said they believed this was a case of Shaken Baby Syndrome. There was no proof that he had did this, but everyone had suspected him. Cherise lost custody of her daughter. The family member that took her daughter in made it easy for her to maintain a relationship with her child, but Marquis was never allowed access to her daughter again.

Things never got better between them after that. She had less time for him, because she worked her full-time job, and then spend several hours after work with her daughter. Their relationship became strained, as her daughter was on another side of town 30 minutes away.

Again, it was a Saturday afternoon when they got into an argument that started in her apartment and went out onto the streets of Euclid Avenue.

I received a phone call that she was in the hospital with head and face injuries. She had been in another physical altercation with him on Euclid Avenue, and had it not been for a passerby Marquis might have killed her right there.

When the man stopped his car and intervened Marquis had slammed Cherise on the concrete face and neck first according to the witness.

The police were most definitely involved, because other people had called the police, and more than one person stopped to help her.

She never could remember what happened, and

maybe that was for the best. I know it disturbed me greatly when I saw her pretty face, and it was scarred up from the gravel that had been embedded in her face.

My friendship with Marquis was over, and I was highly concerned about the safety of Cherise. I wanted her to leave him alone. She was losing everything important to her because of that relationship.

Rent money had been stolen from her purse while she was sleep in her apartment. She wouldn't listen to our reasoning that he had taken some part in that activity. Her relationship with me became so strained that we went from talking 4 to 5 times a day to maybe once a week. My mother however stayed heavily involved with her as much as she could, as if she was her child, and helped to mend our relationship. Things seemed to be getting back to normal we were seeing one other every day and talking a few times a day.

We all carpooled to work, we worked in three different places, but when transportation issues came up, we worked it out for everyone involved to be able to get where they needed to be. Some days we might get to work early, or even have to stay late but we made it happen.

Cherise decided to move from Euclid to

Cleveland to be closer to her daughter. Things were getting back to the way they use to be. She was growing out of that relationship. She was more focused on work and her daughter and she wasn't so into him anymore.

My relationship was not much better, I was in a relationship with a alcoholic. Although he wasn't abusive physically or verbally he was emotionally and financially abusive. This one evening my boyfriend stayed out all night on one of his drinking binges I wanted to get revenge. My plan was to stay at Cherise's apartment overnight, so that he knew what it felt like to be worried all night long. Later that evening I decided against it.

Well as it turned out it would be a night I will forever regret. I never went back to Cherise house, and the activities that took place that evening were life changing for all involved.

I woke up and headed to Cherise house as usual. I got there and called as usual and then went to the door. I beat on the door and called, and even told my mother to call as I continued to knock.

I stood there and listen to the phone ring listening to hear her stir around. In my mind she had over slept.

It wouldn't be the first time this had happened but it was getting close to making us all late.

I left and went and picked up my mother, proceeding with our daily routine. However, we had continuously called until reaching my mother's job.

Once I dropped her off I headed to work also. In route my phone rang. It was Marquis on the other end saying "where is my thang?" I was completely confused because when I left her apartment the night before they were together making plans for their evening.

So I in return said, I thought that she was with you. His response was we got into it last night, I went to my grandmother's house. That was the first red flag for me because every time they had ever gotten into an argument, she would call me or my mother and tell us what happened, and neither of us had heard anything.

I told him that we weren't together and that I was headed to work, I believed that she had overslept. He then asked me if I wanted to go with him to her apartment to wake her up for work. I told him she should be up and on her way to work. I was running late for my job and I would come meet him there so that we could make sure she was up.

Marquis didn't have a key to her apartment so he had to knock on the door just like I did. We went, I threw rocks at the window, called and beat on the door, still no response. I had to get to work. While at

97

work her mother and aunt, that had custody of her daughter called me to see what was going on she had not called off or called into work to say she was going to be late and no one had heard from her.

At that time I made arrangements with her aunt to go by once I could leave work. By noon it was wearing on my spirit that something just wasn't right, I left work, phoned her aunt, and my lil brother Charles, and Marquis, because he had called me several times to see what was going on.

I picked up my lil brother and Marquis walked down the street from his grandparents' house, and Cherise aunt made her way there.

We tried to hoist my lil brother up to her second-floor apartment balcony to look in, so that we didn't have to damage her apartment. They had contacted her landlord for permission to enter and he wouldn't grant it. So at that time Marquis took matters into his own hands. He ran up to the front door of her apartment and busted right into the apartment with his shoulder.

I followed in right behind him. Looking at the surroundings I looked to see if anything looked out of place. She had only been there for a few weeks, and was too busy to unpack, so she was still living out of boxes.

Nothing in the living room and dining room

looked out of place then I heard him run into the ironing board and start screaming. All this taking place within a matter of 10-15 seconds of entering. That's when I spotted her lifeless body lying motionless in the doorway to her bedroom.

I blacked out, when I came back around to the situation an officer had Marquis in a car and my brother Charles was in another car.

Marquis pleaded guilty to aggravated murder and is currently serving 15 years to life. He was denied his first parole attempt.

Cherise, unlike Ava did not get out of her relationship, and was murdered by the very man who spoke of unconditionally loving her, and would do anything to be with her and protect her. It's not enough to know, and see what is wrong, and then take no action, far too many of us take the spectators role, and it's none of my business attitude, and the wait and see approach, until it's too late. When is enough, enough?

Sunglasses: What You Hiding?

Boxing is violent and it's about punishing an opponent. It's not friendly conversation about how their day has been. It's about bringing pain to another human being just for the sport of it, and usually personal financial gain.

Those participating, or paying to see this sport, do so for the brutal enjoyment of witnessing two people physically hurting and injuring one another.

Is this reflective of our country, that we love to see blood and violence, pain and suffering, and want to witness the legal death of someone, is it worth the price of admission?

We boast of being a civilized country, yet we seek violence as entertainment. Is it any wonder that even domestic violence has become no more than entertainment for the masses, where even the courts render decision that some causes are justified under the law?

Some people are going as far as saying, it's okay to beat your partner as long as you don't leave any visible marks on them, and if done correctly, fear will keep them from talking to anyone about it.

The moral values of the country have changed dramatically moving from sensible to senseless, from sympathy to apathy.

Women are fearful in their own homes when it comes to their partners and abuse. They have become good at masking, hiding and covering up the truth, some because of the stigma associated with it, "how could you let something like that happen" to you, "I thought you were smarter than that", " you of all people".

In the boxing ring a battered fighter has to have his face cleaned up and wounds addressed before stepping back in. Battered women do the same before they step back into the world. They hide what has taken place by covering and concealing their bruises with make-up.

Many women choose to hide behind sunglasses as it is one way to hide the shame, embarrassment, and scars associated with abuse.

There are men who won't hesitate to not only hit a woman, but will also take her life if she does not give in the their every whim.

Death might seem extreme, but the threat of it should not be taken lightly.

When emotional threats and intimidation don't get the message across clearly, then the abuser takes it to the next level, and that's physically, as a means to convey their controlling desire.

The emotional scars are lasting, even when the physical bruises vanish, they remain.

Sunglasses are seen as cool and a fashion statement. But they also have the ability to hide eyes of fear, and sadness, and can hide eyes that have been bruised and sleepless.

Sunglasses can become a shield and a wall to hide the pain the abused continues enduring.

Behind the glasses and makeup is a shattered and wounded spirit hurting, and not sure where to find relief.

Victims of abuse think of themselves as unlovable, and unworthy even as they tell others they are valuable.

Most women have this kind of conversation because it's what they are expected to say, and not what they believe. Many women don't want others to think lesser of them, so they hide the truth behind the glasses.

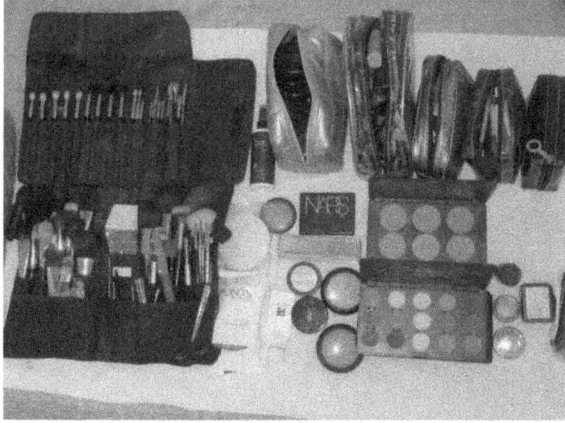

Getting out of a violent and abusive relationship is not easy, as it is an emotional and fear filled process, and requiring help.

The abusers are proud of their actions as a fighter inflicting pain. The abuser sees nothing less than victory and total control.

The greater the pain, the greater the control. Bear in mind also that some women suffering domestic violence will remain hidden behind closed doors until the physical wounds heal, and to hide the fact they are being abused.

Round 12
So, You Broke a Heel?

There's a battle being fought over a matter of equality. That men and women are the same, that they are equal in all they do.

Sadly, this is being promoted as true, when it is in fact not true at all. Now bear in mind that I am not speaking about equal pay for equal work. What I am speaking of here is, the innate differences between the sexes.

We have been born men and women for a designed purpose, and these differences are what makes each of us unique, and we should celebrate these differences.

The male and female bodies differ in look as well as strength, this is mentioned for observation not argumentation.

Now, we hear of weak-minded men, and strong-willed women, and so a new fight has come to the forefront, and that is physical and mental superiority.

Bodies differ, as well as the mind. Men are told to learn to think like a woman, and women are told to learn to think like a man, not for the insight that doing this will give, but for the purpose of reducing and removing the respect that goes with the difference between men and women.

Men, (*some, not all*), feared what was called the liberation of women and began to see them as a threat that would have to be controlled, as not to let them get out of hand. The greatest danger has come from those who have embraced this mindset.

Many women seek independence from men, to have a life and career for themselves. Doing this, it became mentally unsettling for some men as women became workers and possibly co-equal to them in the worlds work force. Remember domestic violence is fear and power based.

When women decided to enter into the ring of life outside the home, many men became disrespectful, inflicting verbal, and physical harassment on the job, so much so this disrespect would also find itself reaching back in their homes as well.

The thinking became, **"it's a man's world"** and

if she wants to be in it she would be treated like any other man.

This belief is where we find many aspects of sexual violence and unwanted sexual advances on the rise in the workplace.

Women working in what was called a man's world was expected to be like the rest of the guys, and for a while they tried to weather that storm to succeed, some women even hiding the verbal disrespect, and shameful touching, to advance or move up the corporate or career ladder.

There were, and continues to be, men who think there is nothing wrong with demeaning women, if their advances are rejected.

Somehow when the woman fights back, she is often put to shame, saying she seduced or encouraged certain actions by dressing a particular way and teasing.

All abuse begins with attacks on the mentality and self-esteem, which at first comes across and thought to be a friendly verbal boxing match, until emotions are elevated.

Men use what they call "FRIENDLY or HARMLESS FLIRTING", fishing for an opportunity to pounce and destroy her or have her terminated should what took place negatively see the light of day.

If she gets in the ring she has to expect to be hit and hit hard, and it will not be pleasant.

When violence, verbal or physical is used it is always thought to be the woman's fault, and why should the abuser be soft on her if she wants to fight. Abusers have to hit her as hard as they would any man that climbs in the ring to stand up against them.

Abusers believe that in order to control a woman, you have to lay your hands on her to show her who's in charge.

Abusers believe they have to remove the woman's will to resist by abuse and violence.

Abusive men also seek to control how "their woman" dresses. He believes that she is drawing attention to herself, and men will notice her, and he feels threatened because of it. She is only allowed to wear what he has approved of. Abusers seek to break the will of their partner in every area of their lives.

Nothing the woman does is about her, but him. For her to change anything about herself is perceived as resisting and challenging his authority.

Round 13
You're Mine

Abusers see people, particularly their partners as personal property and not as individuals. This in their minds takes place the moment they entered into a relationship.

The property minded relationship on the surface does not appear to be so, but it does not take long before this thinking slowly begins to rear its head.

The thinking becomes, they, (their new partner) don't need anyone else in their lives now that they, (the abuser), is now in the relationship. Abusers seek to have their partner completely dependent on them, for every aspect of their lives.

Fighters look for the right opportunity to attack with a flurry of blows against their opponent, to catch them off balance in the hope of finishing the fight through dominance. A time when the opponent's defenses are low, and they are exposed to harm.

Abusers think much in the same way, they seek efficiency, the right moment to do maximum harm.

Seeing another person as personal property is to also believe they have no rights. It's a power play done to make a clear point. And what point is that? Not to question or challenge the abuser or things can get worse.

The beginning actions of abuse catches many women off guard, and they don't immediately know how to respond, possibly believing it was in fact only a one time accident due to emotions.

Violence if ignored on any level, and played down slowly becomes tolerated, and in some cases becomes acceptable behavior.

Culturally we are more attuned to attempting to place blame rather than see violence for what it is and how it impacts lives.

Some people sitting on the sideline, (*outside the ring*) can be heard saying, "maybe they had it coming" or "they deserved what they got". Statements such as these justify the violence, and the attack or the abuse.

Abusers believe they can do anything they feel like doing, because their partner is seen as personal property, and can be treated any way they choose to treat them.

Abusers continue to do so, because they have no fear of consequences, or at the least will be justified for their actions, just as a fighter who is allowed to continue to violently punish their opponent until either the referee or the bell ends it.

Why would someone allow another human being to be punished in such a matter and why would another human being seek to do so? This has been called the 64-thousand-dollar question, but the answer is quite simple, because it's acceptable. It's the mindset as was stated before, of superior and inferior, strong verses the so-called weak.

Men who are hurting, internally often manifest that hurt through visual and physical means in some effort to cope, and deal with it, or to have power over it. It's reverting back to a child, seeking safety and comfort (*I speak more about this in the book: Victims of Bullies domestic violence and children*).

This violent behavior is all about them. What they feel, how they feel, and what they want. And what exactly is it they want? Victory over whatever it is that is tormenting them, and how is this done? By using whatever method, they believe will bring that victory about.

Abusers don't do so because they have to, but because they choose to.

Choice is always an option in anything we choose to do in life, and the choices we make have negative or positive results depending on what we decide to do.

A woman is not a piece of furniture, an object, or there to please and grant a man his every wish.

Historically, women have been seen as an addition to the man's life, and for his exclusive pleasure, and if she gets out of line, discipline would be required whether verbal or physical to get her back in line.

The "you're mine" attitude, stems from how many men were taught to believe a woman's place was in the home, to provide for them, and to be sexual slaves to them whenever called on for sex.

You're mine. You do what I say, when I say, and for as long as I say do it.

We live in a culture where bullying, and violence is accepted as normal behavior, and is now being seen as a problem, one that has existed all along, but ignored until it has become that snowball that has been rolling down the hill, now getting bigger and more dangerous.

It's been thought of as cute, when children are defiant and rebellious, and not taken serious as an issue that will grow up with them, and in them. And becoming not so cute,

Being aggressive and possessive is seen as a good character trait and seen as leadership quality.

Violence is not cute. Abuse is not, and should never be deemed acceptable, and individuals are not property.

Round 14
Throw in the Towel

Some fights become so brutal that the referee steps in and ends the fight before it reaches its conclusion. Then there is the person who is in the corner watching the fight as well. This person likewise has the power to end the fight, by throwing in the towel.

Throwing in the towel in the fight world means the fighter has had enough, the fight has gone to a point that it can become harmful or possibly fatal if allowed to continue.

Why is it that so many women hesitate to throw in the relationship or domestic abuse towel?

For the many onlookers it appears that this is an easy action to comply with. They say, "just do it", "get out and run fast". This is easy to say when you are not the one experiencing the abuse. There are any number of reasons some women remain in abusive relationships.

For instance, some women stay out of **Fear**,

they're afraid of what they believe will happen to them, or their family, if they decide to leave the relationship. Friends and families have been threatened by abusive partners, and for this cause, they may not feel safe leaving.

Some women believe this, (his), behavior of **Abuse, is Normal**: If a woman doesn't know what a healthy relationship looks or feels like because of growing up in an environment where abuse was common, they may not recognize immediately that their relationship is unhealthy.

Afraid of Being Outed: Some women stay because of some unresolved secret in their past held against them and the abuser threatens to reveal this secret to everyone if they leave.

Embarrassment: It's hard for some women to admit that they've been abused often thinking, it's something they have done wrong, and what will their friends think if they found out that they were not as strong as they said they were. Even further, worrying about friends and family judging them.

Low Self-esteem: Abusers will focus on the self-esteem of the woman by way of constant badgering even blaming them for the actions that take place and brought against them. Words that are accompanied by violence, tend to make the abused more receptive.

Love: A woman may stay in an abusive

relationship hoping that their abuser will change because they love them. A promise of love made frequently after violence, accompanied by moments of guilt until the next time. We are taught that "love conquers all", and if we just hang in there it will be alright.

Hope drives some women to believe, that giving the abuser unconditional love, and forgiving them time after time, that hopefully they will change. Sadly, the words do not match the actions.

Many married women who practice religious faith, believe God disapproves of divorce, and so they remain in abusive relationships, as if it is God's will for them.

Some women believe that if they stay "prayed up" and prayerfully surrender to the abuser, things will change because they don't want the relationship to end, but only the abuse.

It is not the will of God that anyone be abused; Think about it, the woman's body is the house of continued life and to abuse it is to possibly end that ability to produce life.

Women continue to suffer the abuse on almost every level, and refuse to throw in the towel for what they call love.

Those in the ring of violence don't see clearly, so

it becomes necessary for someone outside to interject some sensibility, and do what they can to end the cycle of continued abuse.

To get out of some relationships requires help and the willingness to accept it. Today there are many resources available for those who are suffering from domestic violence and some of them are included in this book.

Throwing in the towel does not mean you are giving up on life but letting go of a toxic relationship. It's deciding that you are priceless not worthless.

Throwing in the towel is not a show of weakness but power. It's the power to make positive changes in your life effective immediately.

Seeing the signs of abuse is not enough to end it, no more than watching a fighter being beat while staggering before falling into unconsciousness. Enough is enough and we must stop sugar coating acts of aggression, and violence as being normal, and acceptable.

Throwing in the towel means having outside help, and that others see the need to intervene and take an active role in helping to end the brutality that has been witnessed.

Domestic violence is not about winners and losers but abuse.

Throwing in the towel does not mean you have given up but waken up. The abused might not have the power to throw in the towel, and take control of their life at the moment. It might seem difficult but it's not impossible.

Throwing in the towel is seen by some, and considered by others as outside interference, but it's getting involved, and no longer being a witness to what has been taking place right in front of them. It's not a sign of quitting but safety.

The abused say they can't take it anymore. But are not always sure what action would be most appropriate and when.

Domestic violence requires community help, and unconditional love, to help a victim overcome this cycle of pain and violence.

Throwing in the towel comes for some, when they, **1**) think of what has taken place in their past, the hurt and pain they have endured through the years beginning from a time in their childhood, **2**) when they remind themselves of present action that keeps them bound as mental and physical prisoners in a toxic relationship, and **3**) thinking about the loss of their identities and self-worth.

In the Ring with Heels On

Throwing in the towel is the best thing that can happen to someone being abused, it's not a negative thing, but a great demonstration of power. It's better to walk away wounded than to be carried away unconscious or dead.

These words are not meant to instill fear, but to encourage change, swift and immediate.

Round 15
The Winner Is

Some fights seem to last for what might seem to be a lifetime when it comes to their brutality, but the rules say they cannot go past 15 rounds, and should they last the full time then a decision will be made based on the number of blows landed or how many times an opponent might have been knocked down to help decide the victor.

In as much as we live in a culture that spouts winners and losers, who's the winner and who's the loser when it comes to domestic violence? Who is it that decides for the victim of abuse how much they should take, or when it should end? Of course, we say there is no winner, and that everybody loses.

We promote violence on a grand scale in almost every aspect of our lives, music, videos, movies, and television. The message is so overwhelmingly clear, that we find road rage and bullying ranking high as methods of solving differences.

Every fight comes to a conclusion but at what cost?

Some fights, not limited to a ring, can last longer than others (weeks, months, years and lifetimes), and can be physically exhausting. There are screams and jeers by those who bet on their favorite fighter to win. Why did it take so long, it should have ended long ago some question?

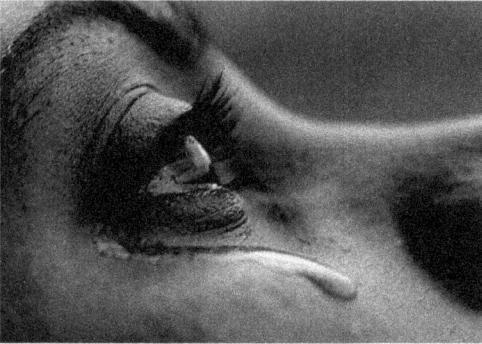

The crowd is now waiting to know who is declared the victor, and who will be given the title winner.

Clearly from the blood and towels used to cover up what seems to be a battered face and body there can only be one clear winner as the fighters stand waiting.

Many women and their friends have attempted to play the role of personal physician. They have worked on themselves to hide, mask and cover up the bruises and marks that have been a regular part of their relationship, and emotionally blame themselves for what has happened to them or for what they continue to endure.

Stepping into the battle ring of life and relationships is to take your life in your hands. Having no idea of the potential outcome of doing so, but, we can take precautions, and measured steps to guide us as safely as possible on our journey from abuse.

All it takes is one blow, emotional or physical and a life can be cut short or someone could be disabled the rest of their life.

Is this or any fight avoidable, and do they have to take place at all? In the mind of some they say yes, they had to learn for themselves life lessons, and declaring they had to make their own mistakes.

Sometimes we reject good advice, desiring to see and experience things for ourselves (*not always a wise thing to do*), but some of the best lessons come by learning from the mistakes of others not duplicating them.

The strong verses the weak, domestic and other violence is part of a particular mindset. It's based on fear, intimidation, control, absolute power and "I must be first mentality".

Getting what is wanted at any cost. Winning is competing for a position ahead of someone else, no matter what needs to be done to achieve it.

Lets' also be mindful that when it comes to domestic violence, it affects a number of areas.

There is **1)** mental abuse, there is **2)** physical abuse, **3)** financial abuse, and there is **4)** sexual abuse, with each having a diverse effect on the individual on the receiving end.

So, when it comes to domestic violence, who is the real winner? When someone is emotionally or physically violated, that's not a win and should not be seen as such.

Most individuals have good intentions, and will advise saying, "get out", "run", get as far away from the pain as possible. But do nothing to help, or get involved, sighting that it's none of their business. But we have seen in the last chapter it will take personal involvement to effectively change matters.

Consider the work of an enabler. They see something is wrong, and do nothing to change it or get involved.

What we accept, we will protect. For many, it's a matter of not taking a side, but watching to see what will happen, and be quietly judgmental. Maybe the winner is the dead woman, and the incarcerated man the loser, problem solved.

Where there are relationships there will also be disagreements. I have not met anyone who agrees all the time on everything, but that does not mean disagreements should escalate and turn to violence.

Love is not abuse, and it's not about remaining in a relationship because you believe somehow the emotional and physical abuse was unintended.

Relationships are not about survival, they're about learning to love, and being loved. There is a time when it becomes necessary to throw in the towel, and end a relationship, but, when is that some have asked?

The moment it becomes clear that things are being done to isolate you from family and friends, and the moment abuse is done, no matter how small it might appear, it will always lead to more abuse, emotional, physical or sexual.

People are not property and should not be treated as such under any circumstance.

Let's be very careful when dealing with emotions as they can lead us to make decisions that can become harmful, because of desire of physical comforts or status, and clouding the mind to what is evidently clearly set before us.

Some violence continues, demanding a decision of power be made. But who decides this and when? No matter how much information is made available, it does no good if that information is denied or simply ignored.

If a fighter turns around and walks away the crowd will not like it, as they are in attendance with expectation. But life decisions should not be made to make the crowd happy, but to be happy personally.

This fight, or refusal to do so is to take control of an individual life action, knowing that it's better to walk away than to be carried away.

The bigger person is the one who is willing to walk away from a fight than to engage in a bout when it's not necessary, or bring undue stress and pain into their life.

This fight of life is not about winning but wisdom. So, who is the real winner here, it's the hospitals, funeral homes and cemeteries?

Entering into a ring is done so at the expense of putting one's health, and possibly life in jeopardy. It is with the expectation of winning, hearing the announcer say those words many long to here, AND THE WINNER IS. But at what cost?

Locker Room

In the ring with heels on. A close, and personal look at what happens when domestic violence becomes normal behavior. Inside the square circle as it is sometimes called, is found unregulated, though it's claimed otherwise, and unbridled abuse and violence. This violence is now found in the home, as well as on the job.

One of the hardest things to accept sometimes is this simple truth.

The truth reveals who, and what we are, and even why we do the things we do in this culture.

This ring is not one that is found on television or pay-per-view.

The ring I am referring to is the one many women almost every waking moment of their day enter.

This ring consists of the four walls of our homes and is often one of the most secretly violent places on earth. It's the place many horrible secrets have been kept hidden from the eyes and ears of family and friends.

Domestic violence is a product of evil desires that fill the heart. Instead of seeing this as an evil action, it's labeled, and promoted as some kind of new disease that only afflict certain groups of people leaving others immune.

Finally, this fact. Everyone is subject to violence regardless of their background, and this takes place on many levels no matter the age race or sex. Violence is invited into our homes, as it is promoted and advertised on a regular basis.

How do we illuminate, and eliminate this cycle of violent action, and can it be controlled? Domestic violence is a serious matter, often a matter of life and death.

We can change this pattern of behavior but don't expect this decision to be popular, especially with those who are abusers.

Violence has become embedded in our culture as the best way to handle disagreements, but we must not continue this action.

As the fighters enter into their locker rooms, they review the events that have taken place, and must do a self-evaluation of what they did in the ring before to either bring them a loss or a victory.

Handlers, promoters, and even the fighter, all have something to say about what took place.

Victims of domestic and other violence must now

have the boldness to speak up on their own behalf and remove the mental fear that often disables them.

No matter what is said to them, it will never be as important as what they will ultimately say to themselves, about themselves.

About the Author

Timothy White Sr. has impacted thousands of people throughout the world as an author, teacher, motivational speaker and minister. Mr. White is on a mission to positively influence millions of people through his work, ministry and writing, which currently exceeds 80+ books covering a plethora of topics including bullying, domestic violence, self-help, history and spirituality.

The Cleveland, Ohio native, a father of five, has overcome many adversities in his life including homelessness and losing his beloved wife to cancer in 1994. Through much heartache and disappointments he discovered a new purpose and passion to use writing as a tool to "plant positive seeds."

Mr. White has developed profound spiritual insight into relationships over the years. Mr. White has written multiple books on the topic of abuse including, *In the Ring with Heels On*, *She's the Boss and Victims of Bullies*. Mr. White writes about these and other issues because of the relevance, and prevalence of domestic and other violence. He believes that, **"Information plus application equals transformation."**

Mr. White is an Evangelist and former pastor. He believes, "God chooses who He uses." He writes, speaks, and ministers to local, national, and international audiences. With an additional 15 new books in the works, Mr. White hopes to give people plenty of "spiritual food" to eat.

White is one of the producers of the documentary ***"Where's Gina?"*** about missing children on which he was also narrator.

He is a co-developer of a tech company (Gsys LLC) that brought blindside technology to vehicles that made billions for the industry, saving countless lives. He is currently co-hosting a radio show,

"Healing the Hurt" on WERE 1490am in Cleveland, Ohio on Thursday evenings 8-10 pm with Host, Rev. Brenda Ware-Abrams.

He is currently on the Advisory Board and is a volunteer instructor at the Juvenile Correction centers in Warrensville Heights and Cleveland, Ohio where his book *Seven Signs of Success* is being taught. His book *Victims of Bullies* is, currently, in the City of Cleveland School system to help stop and make aware of solutions to the issue of bullying.

timwhite55@gmail.com   Timwhitepublishing.com

www.ingramcontent.com/pod-product-compliance
Lightning Source LLC
Chambersburg PA
CBHW021238090426
42740CB00006B/588